Chris is an award-winning arts leader, artistic director, playwright, programmer, producer and dramaturg. He is currently Artistic Director of the iconic Bondi Pavilion in Sydney and was Director and CEO of Critical Stages Touring, connecting outstanding professional theatre and live performance with regional and metropolitan audiences across Australia and New Zealand (2014- 2022). He was previously Guest Curator of the 2013 National Play Festival for Playwriting Australia; Artistic Director and CEO of Deckchair Theatre (2008-2012) in WA; Artistic Director of Theatre@Risk in Melbourne (2001-2007); and Resident Director at Melbourne Theatre Company (2002-2006).

He won the WA Equity Award for Best Director in 2009 and 2011 and was nominated for a Green Room Award for Outstanding Direction in 2001. He was awarded the Queen's Trust Australia and Foundation for Young Australians Centenary Grant (2001), the George Fairfax Memorial Award for Theatre (2003), and a Goethe Institut / Playwriting Australia Dramaturgy Fellowship (2008).

Previous writing highlights include: *The Lonely Hearts Club* (with Cathy Travers, Deckchair Theatre); *Lorelei* (with Mark Storen, Deckchair Theatre); and *Babel Towers* (co-created with Polash Larsen and ensemble. theatre@risk).

Highlights as a director include: *Thomas Murray and the Upside Down River* by Reg Cribb (Griffin Theatre and NORPA 2016, Critical Stages national tour 2018; *Stones in his Pockets* (Critical Stages NSW tour 2015/16, national tour 2017). For Deckchair Theatre productions include: *The Magic Hour* by Vanessa Bates (Nominated for Drover Award for Tour of the Year 2014, Performing Lines National Tour, including Queensland Theatre Company and Darwin Festival); *Taking Liberty* (WA Equity Award nominations Best Production and Best Director 2012); *The Modern International Dead* (WA Equity Award Winners Best Director and Best Production 2011); *Grace* adapted from the novel by Robert Drewe (Perth International Arts Festival 2010); *Checklist for an Armed Robber* by Vanessa Bates (WA Equity Award Winner Best Director 2009).

BLACK/BLOOD
SUN/MOON

Chris Bendall

CURRENCY PLAYS

First published in 2022
by Currency Press
Gadigal Land, PO Box 2287 Strawberry Hills, NSW, 2012, Australia
enquiries@currency.com.au
www.currency.com.au

in association with Critical Stages Touring.

Published in this edition 2024.

Typeset by Brighton Gray for Currency Press.
Printed by Fineline Print + Copy Services, Revesby, NSW.
Cover illustration by Adam Niescioruk and Robbi James.
Cover design by Hayden Rodgers.

Currency Press acknowledges the Traditional Owners of the Country on which we live and work. We pay our respects to all Aboriginal and Torres Strait Islander Elders, past and present.

A catalogue record for this
book is available from the
National Library of Australia

Contents

Playwright's Note

This story was inspired by my own daughter, whose climate activism and passion very much formed the basis of the character of Maddy. As described in the early scenes of the play, it stemmed from a conversation I had with her, when I unwittingly revealed to her that what we currently call a Climate Emergency, has been a concern of scientists for at least 4 decades now. The betrayal she so keenly felt, that an entire generation had failed to act in time to protect her future was palpable, and heartbreaking.

My own relatively feeble token gestures which were limited mostly to keyboard activism on social media suddenly seemed appallingly slight in the face of the seemingly impossible task ahead, and the likely terrible future impact on my children and their generation. So, the genesis of this play actually came very much from conversations with her, her own growing activism and especially attending school strikes with her. The seeds of the play grew further over the summer of 2019/2020 with the horrendous bushfires across Australia.

This play is based on close and careful research into climate change and its impact on Australia and the globe, as well as current knowledge of what can be done to mitigate these impacts and protect our future generations. It is also based on research into the state of Australia's current legal system especially regarding juvenile justice, and the current age of criminal responsibility at just 10 years of age in Australia.

But the play is also a fantasy and a celebration of the power of storytelling and the imagination. I wanted the play to offer hope, and so there are two storylines. While Maddy's storyline is closely embedded in fact and research, the other storyline follows the path of Katie, originally a climate denier, and her journey of literal flights of fancy as I attempt to imagine a magical solution to the crisis.

This has been a passion project for me for the past three years, and I hope that the work can inspire those that watch it, to follow their own path to learn more about the role that they can play to meet the challenges ahead of us. I also hope that one day, this play will be no more than a history piece about the challenges that faced our country and our globe, and how we imagined our way out of them before the tipping point, and before we met the crisis head on and changed our society, our politics, and our ways of thinking for the better

Chris Bendall

Playwright
1 May 2022

For Eloise and Isobel

Black Sun / Blood Moon was first produced by Critical Stages Touring at The Playhouse Theatre, Wagga Wagga, on 20 May, 2022, with the following cast:

MADDY	Adelaide Kennedy
PAUL	Garth Holcombe
KATIE	Francesca Savige
TINO / ADRIAN / POLICE OFFICER	Tommy Misa

Director, Chris Bendall
Set and Costume Designer, Isla Shaw
Lighting Designer, Becky Russell
Sound Designer, Kingsley Reeve
Video Designer, Susie Henderson
Puppetry Director, Alice Osborne
Dramaturg, Hilary Bell

Its national tour was produced by Critical Stages Touring, beginning at Cairns Performing Arts Centre, QLD, on 14 April, 2023, with the following cast:

MADDY	Adelaide Kennedy / Eloise Bendall
PAUL / SOLVEIG	Matthew Whittet
KATIE	Francesca Savige
TINO / ADRIAN / POLICE OFFICER	Lani Tupu

‘As yet the wind is an untamed and unharnessed force; and quite possibly one of the greatest discoveries hereafter to be made will be the taming and harnessing of it.’—Abraham Lincoln, 1860

‘I’d put my money on the sun and solar energy, what a source of power. I just hope we don’t have to wait until oil and coal run out before we tackle that.’—Thomas Edison, 1931

‘We shall need a substantially different way of thinking, if humanity is to survive.’—Albert Einstein, 1949

‘When the last tree is cut, the last fish is caught, and the last river is polluted; when to breathe the air is sickening, you will realise, too late, that wealth is not in bank accounts and that you can’t eat money.’—Alanis Obomsawin, 1972

‘Any sufficiently advanced technology is indistinguishable from magic.’—Arthur C. Clarke, 1973

‘Our planet is a lonely speck in the great enveloping cosmic dark. In our obscurity, in all this vastness, there is no hint that help will come from elsewhere to save us from ourselves.’—Carl Sagan, 1994

‘Surely we have a responsibility to leave for future generations a planet that is healthy and habitable by all species.’—David Attenborough, 2002

‘Dear future generations: please accept our apologies. We were rolling drunk on petroleum.’—Kurt Vonnegut, 2006

‘And since our time is running out we have decided to take action. We have started to clean up your mess and we will not stop until we are done.’—Greta Thunberg, 2020

CHARACTERS

PAUL, mid-40s male

MADDY, ten- to twelve-year-old girl

KATIE, mid-30s female

TINO, Samoan male

ADRIAN, lawyer, male

SOLVEIG, seventy-year-old Norwegian woman

POLICE OFFICER, mid-30s

SHAHIN, a peregrine falcon

POLAR BEAR, SIBERIAN TIGER, GORILLA, SAND GAZELLES, ANDEAN DEAR, BILBY, PINK COCKATOO, ROCK WALLABY, DOLPHIN

NOTES

Intended to be performed by four actors.

The same actor should play TINO, POLICE OFFICER and ADRIAN.

PAUL should also play SOLVEIG.

The cast should reflect the diversity of Australia.

/ marks the point where the line is interrupted by the next speaker.

dialogue in brackets ( ) is unspoken.

… means the character hesitates or trails off.

The play begins in January 2020 in Australia and takes place over approximately two years, which includes the period of the COVID-19 global pandemic.

The production moves through many locations throughout, but should never be too fixed in any one location. A minimalist, transformative production aesthetic is strongly encouraged. Given the subject matter, recycled materials and a sustainable approach to design are also requested.

This isn't a work for audiences to sit back and passively enjoy. The success of the production will hinge on the production team's ability to involve audience members directly as much as possible throughout.

ACT ONE

SCENE ONE

PAUL, *alone on stage, addresses the audience.*

PAUL: So my daughter, at the age of ten, attended her first climate strike.

Beat.

She's worried. We all are, aren't we? Well those of us who believe the science. Who choose to listen to the science. Who believe it's in our power to do something, anything, about the science.

Beat.

So a ten-year-old girl strikes.

She was one of the youngest but her voice was as loud as the rest as they marched down the main street of Wagga Wagga, right up to the minister's office.

But now.

Beat.

After the endless drought and years with no rain, now ash is raining down on us. Family homes … just embers. And our wildlife? Billions of animals they say … The scale of it all … I just can't … A black summer indeed.

Beat.

Is this what we are all just supposed to get used to now? Drought. Fire. Dead fish in our rivers.

Pause.

Dead fish in our rivers.

It's like Mother Nature just got so pissed off with the lot of us—the whole country—that she just needed to give us this massive slap in the face. Slap. Slap. Slap. 'Wake up, you dumb nuts. Stop sleepwalking your way to oblivion!'

But will it work? Will we wake up? Will we listen?

What a mess our generation is handing to our children.

I heard this the other day …

Two planets meet. The first one asks: 'How are you?'

'Not so well,' the second answered, 'I've got the Homo Sapiens.'

'Don't worry,' the other replied, 'I had that once. They won't last long.'

Sorry. Dad climate joke.

One day, some time last year, I'm sitting chattering away with Maddy—that's my daughter. We were playing a board game—snakes and ladders, I think.

And we were talking about books. Her favourites now, and mine when I was her age … She's devouring the Harry Potter series—of course. 'Expecto Patronum!'

One of mine was this one …

He walks over to pick a book up from a shelf in the room or perhaps just scattered on the floor.

Douglas Adams' *The Hitchhiker's Guide to the Galaxy* … Anyone read it?

He smiles, clasping the book to his chest.

Recently I'd been thinking about the moment in the book where the dolphins flee from Earth forever leaving one final message: 'So long and thanks for all the fish.' I was wondering if it could have been a bit of a nod to early days of learning about the threat of climate change, with dolphins smart enough to see it was time to get out while the going was good … Anyway, I was thinking all this out loud when I realise what I'm revealing to her. I was talking about someone old—and I mean actually old, not just Dad old, but way older than me—we're talking about a book written in 1979—before I was even born.

MADDY *appears.*

MADDY: So you're telling me that people knew? Before you were even born?

PAUL: Maybe longer.

MADDY: And that—what—they didn't do anything?

PAUL: Well. Maybe not nothing.

But not enough.

MADDY: Clearly not enough!

PAUL: No not enough. Not nearly enough. You know there have been a lot of people trying though. Investigating the causes. Around the world … I mean we did fix the ozone layer.

MADDY: The what?

PAUL: Long story. Look—point is—it's not that people haven't been trying. It's just—it's a big challenge … It's going to take some time.

[*To the audience*] But it's 2020. And there's a young girl watching her future disappear in a cloud of carbon emissions.

And so then—it comes …

MADDY: [*anger building*] So if you've known all this time. Then—what have you done? What have you been doing all this time?

PAUL: [*to himself*] What have I done … What have I done … [*To the audience*] To save the world? To protect our planet? My daughter's future? My grandchildren not yet born? … Not enough that's for sure.

MADDY: [*furiously*] I hate you, Dad. You're the worst!

PAUL: And I think of this as the moment when it all began. When she disappeared into this cloud. Because this has been our ultimate betrayal, hasn't it? We did this—my generation. Not just our parents or our grandparents or our political leaders. Sure it goes right back to the British—doesn't everything?— and the start of the industrial revolution. But it was *our* responsibility.

Pause.

Maddy and I live together in our small house just outside of Wagga Wagga. So good they named it twice.

MADDY: [*rolling her eyes*] Dad …

PAUL: When I was growing up people said it meant the place of many crows. But in the local Wiradjuri language, it means the place where people come to dance and celebrate. Not that much dancing lately. Air pollution here over the summer was one of the worst in the whole state—far worse than anything those Sydney-siders were whinging about …

We're about five hundred kilometres southwest-ish from Sydney and a couple of hundred from Canberra. It's a university town. I lecture in English literature.

When she was younger I used to tell her stories at night. Find ourselves riding on the back of dolphins discovering hidden worlds, deep in the ocean, where an underwater lobster band might be found playing [*singing*] 'Under the sea!'

But that was then. And now … She was looking for inspiration, for a role model … She starts to search for books on climate change and climate activists. Greta [*pronouncing her name incorrectly 'Thun-Berg'*] Thunberg …

MADDY: It's pronounced Toon-berg, Dad.

PAUL: Maddy was in awe of Greta …

MADDY: Toon-berg.

PAUL: Thanks.

Beat.

Greta threatened the establishment. She threatened the dinosaurs. The corrupt. The inept. And she spoke her mind.

MADDY: [*holding a book about Greta*] 'We will be a pain in the arse and keep striking.'

MADDY *passes the book to a member of the audience.*

[*To an audience member*] Hi—can you just read this part for us?

AUDIENCE ONE: 'I have learned that you are never too small to make a difference.'

MADDY: Thanks! [*Taking the book back*] Do you believe that's true, Dad? Can anyone actually make a difference?

PAUL: Of course I do—it doesn't matter if you are ten or one hundred and ten. You have to believe that anything is possible, Maddy. 'Even the smallest person can change the course of the future.' That's Tolkien.

MADDY: Okay …?

PAUL: Now—what do we need to get ready for your first day back at school tomorrow?

MADDY: Can I take in this book about Greta?

PAUL: Sure thing.

Beat.

[*To the audience*] So after the summer from hell, she goes back to school ready for action, inspired and bold. She was ready to talk with her friends about what they could do together. Start a newspaper, create a movement, make some noise.

[*To* MADDY] How was school? What did you all talk about? Are you all working out how to save the planet?

MADDY: I don't know … They just all want to play Minecraft!

PAUL: [*to the audience*] Had everyone already forgotten checking air quality and smoke levels all summer? Not being able to go out to play or even open a window? Did we all just get used to a sun so shrouded in smoke that you could look right at it? In the day—a black sun. And at night—a moon glowing blood red from the fires. Insta-worthy sunsets every day … Mementos to our downfall.

MADDY: It's like summer never happened.

PAUL: And she loses confidence. Deflates. Little by little.

[*To* MADDY] How was school today?

MADDY: Fine.

PAUL: What did you all talk about?

MADDY: I've got homework to do, Dad.

PAUL: [*to the audience*] Story time …

[*To* MADDY] Once upon a time there was a young girl. A girl whose town is being threatened by a great *environmental* catastrophe. But she is a girl who has extraordinary gifts and she starts to hear voices. So she follows those voices across the oceans and into an enchanted forest where she learns of a great wrong committed many years ago /

MADDY: Dad—I know that's just the story of *Frozen Two*.

PAUL: [*to the audience*] It was worth a try. So the next night I try again …

[*To* MADDY] There was once a girl who loved to disobey authority, including her parents, and when her island was suffering and the fish were dying—

MADDY: *Moana* now? Don't you know any stories other than Disney ones?

PAUL: Okay okay, sorry. There just aren't any new stories anymore! So let's steal honestly next time. I'll recycle some stories. From history.

MADDY *groans.*

What? I thought you wanted me to be recycling more.

MADDY: Really, Dad?

PAUL: [*to the audience*] So for the next few nights I tell her about some real heroes: Mahatma Gandhi, Martin Luther King, Rosa Parks.

[*To an audience member, passing them a book about Mandela*] Actually, can you read this for me?

AUDIENCE TWO: 'Education is the most powerful weapon which you can use to change the world.'

PAUL: Mandela.

MADDY *grabs the book and exits to read it.*

So perhaps it was my fault. Perhaps my primer in non-violent civil disobedience was just a little premature … Did I dream of her growing up and saving the planet? Sure. Doesn't every parent want their child to be a real-life superhero?

Beat.

But was I prepared for the consequences?

MADDY *walks in carrying a sign. She sits in the centre of the stage and holds the sign in front of her. It reads: 'Unless someone like you cares a whole awful lot. Nothing is going to get better. It's not. Dr Seuss.'*

Blackout.

Music.

News footage blasts across the stage.

Fire.

Flood.

Drought.

SCENE TWO

On a street in Wagga Wagga. It's hot.

MADDY *is still sitting on stage with her sign.* KATIE *walks past on her way into her office.*

KATIE: And what do you think you're doing here?

MADDY: I'm protesting. Hashtag Fridays for Future.

KATIE: Great, but do you have to do that here? You're kind of in our way.

MADDY: There's a climate emergency. It's kind of in the way of my future.

KATIE: So what exactly do you want me to do about that?

MADDY: I want you to *do something*!
KATIE: Good to know. I'll keep that in mind.

KATIE walks past the protester and into her office. The office of Jacqueline Thompson MP, federal member for the Riverina. Katie's phone rings.

[*Answering phone*] No comment

She hangs up. Another call.

[*Answering*] I said no comment.

She hangs up again. TINO arrives.

TINO: Excuse me.
KATIE: No, I'm sorry, Ms Thompson isn't seeing anyone today.
TINO: Oh that's okay, actually it's you I …
KATIE: Oh God help me, you're not another eco-warrior are you? Thank you but I don't have time for any more of you today. We have a comments box by the door or you can go to the minister's website. [*Fake smiling*] Goodbye, thank you for visiting.
TINO: No no you don't / understand I just—
KATIE: [*through clenched teeth*] Goodbye.

She ushers him out the door. TINO has no choice but to leave. She sees that MADDY is still sitting outside her office.

Are you still here? Go home, kid. Go home.

A sudden burst of wind. Some rubbish blows at KATIE's feet. She tries to kick it away, but a piece of paper catches her eye, so she takes a closer look and stares at it for a long time before shoving it in her pocket.

Lunatic greenies.

SCENE THREE

Maddy and Paul's home.

PAUL: Hey, Maddy, are you ready for school? Time to go!

> MADDY *enters—not in uniform, but holding a new sign: 'I can't go to school, I have to save the planet.' It's decorated with flowers and trees.*

What's this?

MADDY: I've made a new sign—like it?

PAUL: I love it but … where's your school uniform?

MADDY: It's Friday, Dad?

PAUL: Oh. Sorry. I thought … You're going again? Aren't you missing out on a bit too much / school now …

MADDY: Dad—I thought you were with me on this? Every Friday until /

PAUL: Until something is done. Yes I know, I know, but … it's been a month. Don't you think it's time to—

MADDY: What?

PAUL: You know—take a break? Let it go for a bit?

MADDY: 'Let it go?' Dad, are you serious?

PAUL: Okay okay. Easy. But—it is a school day—I don't want you to get behind in your / classes.

MADDY: [*temper flaring*] We agreed that I just have to keep up with my school work! I'm off, Dad. I don't want to be late for the others.

PAUL: Hold on—just—wait—I might need to check in with your mother about this? I don't want her /

MADDY: Dad—it's fine. Mum knows.

PAUL: And?

MADDY: And she's fine with it …

> *Beat.*

[*Patience wearing thin*] She's fine with it, Dad …?

> *Pause.*

> MADDY *stares at him.*

PAUL: [*defensively*] Okay!
Okay okay okay.

[*Soothingly*] Sorry, Maddy. I just … I just worry about you is all. All by yourself.

MADDY: I'm not by myself, Dad. Lily's with me. And Bridget. And Charlie.

PAUL: Great. I'll come and pick you up after my lectures. Good luck!

MADDY: Thanks, Dad!

SCENE FOUR

KATIE *in her office. Working.*

Another paper appears at her feet—a paper crane.

KATIE: [*reading*] 'Time is running out. We need to talk. Meet me at Romano's … ' Scammers … When are they going to give up?

She exits.

SCENE FIVE

On the street in Wagga Wagga. MADDY *and* PAUL *both hold signs.*

MADDY: How cool was that, Dad?

PAUL: [*to the audience*] Another climate rally.

MADDY: Thanks for coming with me.

PAUL: Well, I care too! It's not just your generation that's worried.

MADDY: Yeah, so how come you've left it all up to us to fix then?

PAUL: Okay okay, fair point.

MADDY *studies him for a moment.*

[*To the audience*] Each week she's joined at her protest by a few more kids, but it's still just a handful. Maybe five or six on a good day.

MADDY: [*leading the crowd in a chant*] What do we want? Climate action! When do we want it? Now!

PAUL: People throw coins at them sometimes.

MADDY: Hey, I'm not a busker!

PAUL: Others just tell them to get out of their way.

MADDY: I've got a right to be here as much as you do!

PAUL: Jacqueline Thompson MP, federal member for the Riverina, sends one of her staffers out every so often.

KATIE: [*passing by*] Look, kid. Right now everyone is busy dealing with the fires. Now is not the time.

PAUL: But mostly they're way too easy to ignore—it's a lovely view of the lagoon from Thompson's office but not that much foot traffic. So they move further down Fitzmaurice Street and set up outside the Court House.

KATIE: Bye, kids. Happy protesting!

MADDY: [*to an audience member*] Hi. Can you spare some time to help me save the world?

PAUL: People keep joining. Some kids are grabbing musical instruments from home or school and the Friday protests becomes quite an event. Which attracts more kids.

MADDY: Our children will ask us. Which side are you on? Part of the solution? Or part of the con.

PAUL: So that when school goes back, it's not just a handful anymore. It's almost half the kids in years five and six. And perhaps some of them were just doing it to skip school. And some of them were doing it just to hang with their friends. But they showed up.

MADDY *leads the crowd and tries to engage the audience in it too. Maybe she brings a couple of people on stage to join her protest here.*

MADDY *continues her chant.*

MADDY: When the climate is under attack what do we do? Stand up! Fight back!

KATIE: [*exploding*] Will you shut up!

SCENE SIX

PAUL *addresses the audience.*

PAUL: Maddy's new Friday school strike spot is catching some attention, but she decides she still needs a bigger audience for her protests so she tries out a new tactic. She gets mobile.

MADDY: Your coffee cup is killing green sea turtles!

PAUL: Protesting *outside* cafes …

MADDY: Where's your keep cup?

PAUL: *Inside* cafes …

MADDY: Don't you know where those plastic straws will end up?

PAUL: At the supermarket …

MADDY: Do you really need to drive up here just to buy that one roll of toilet paper?

PAUL: Even yelling at passing cars from the street!

MADDY: Why do you need such a huge car for one person? Think of the planet!

PAUL: Shaming the whole town.

MADDY: Why are you even driving? Ride a bike!

PAUL: Like Cassandra—*cursed* with the gift of foresight, but /

MADDY: WHY IS NO-ONE LISTENING TO ME?

PAUL: As she warns the world of its imminent destruction.

SCENE SEVEN

MADDY *sits on the street with a new sign: 'There is no Planet B.'*

KATIE: You're back?

MADDY: It's Friday.

KATIE: Look, I'm just not sure what you think we can do here. We are such a tiny proportion of the world's population! Like a tiny grain of rice in a Chinese banquet. You don't seriously think anything we do here in the Riverina is going to make the slightest difference, do you?

MADDY: We may be only a small percentage of the world's total population, but every one of us is releasing about seventeen tonnes of carbon pollution each year! More than three times the average person on the planet.

KATIE: Look, our government is doing all it can at this time. We're investing in real solutions.

MADDY: But that's not true, is it?

KATIE: What isn't true?

MADDY: You aren't investing in 'real solutions'—not like renewable energy. That's real. And there is way more we could be doing. Like not burning fifty million barrels of coal—every day—for a start.

KATIE: Sounds to me like you're just making things up / now.

TINO *appears in the background and he begins filming their conversation.*

MADDY: I'm not making this up. These are statistics. It's science. What we do here does make a difference to the world. Why can't you /

KATIE: I think it's time for more learning and less activism, young / lady.

MADDY: You're all acting like we can solve this sometime in the future—like we'll get to net zero by 2050, by letting someone else do something in 2049. But if we wait until then—it's going to be too late.

KATIE: Look, it's not as simple as that.

MADDY: Didn't you see the fires? Can't you see what's happening to the world? Why can't you see it the way I see it?

KATIE: Okay, I've had enough now. You've had your fun. When will you get it into your head that no-one cares? We just don't care!

KATIE *kicks the sign out of the way.* TINO *walks away, smiling.*

PAUL: [*to the audience*] Someone caught the exchange on their phone. It went viral.

SCENE EIGHT

A bar. KATIE *pulls up a high bar stool. She pulls out of her pocket the piece of paper that she found earlier and stares at the message on it.*

KATIE: What are you looking at? Just said what everyone else was thinking, if you ask me … Now isn't the time, is it? There's enough to deal with already without all the greenie nutters.

[*To another audience member*] So it's hotter this year—next year it will be cooler. Things change, don't they? Lost my job now. I guess that's changed.

She lights a cigarette. She sees TINO *watching her. He takes a step towards her.*

What—you again.

TINO: Hello.

KATIE: You lot—if you're not demanding more bike lanes and chanting two wheels good, four wheels bad, then you're stomping your feet for more electric car charging stations—and telling us we should all be driving a Tesla or something!

TINO: [*walking towards her with his hand outstretched to introduce himself*] I think you've got me confused for /

KATIE: Just get on your bike and get out of here.

TINO: I really need to talk.

He steps forward suddenly and as KATIE *stumbles back she knocks into a customer at the bar.*

KATIE: Hey—Don't come near me.

She leaves the bar. It's very windy outside. TINO *follows her.*

Who *are* you …? Are you following me?

She picks up her phone and dials a number.

[*Pressing her phone to her ear*] Please pick up please pick up …

Newspapers, debris and dust sweep onto the stage. A piece of paper wraps itself round her leg and she picks it up.

[*Reading*] 'Trust him … A car will arrive shortly … Follow the map … ' What map? What the—

TINO: Please—You need to come with me /

KATIE: Stay back!

She tries to duck away from him.

TINO: [*walking to her, hand outstretched*] Our car has arrived. We will stop by your house to collect a few essentials. But we need to leave now.

KATIE: [*into her phone*] Please pick up please pick up please pick up …

TINO: Please take this. It will help explain things.

A metallic tablet drops to the stage as if from nowhere, resembling an iPad, but not quite. She taps the screen and it lights up in her hands.

The lunar eclipse is coming, Miss Katie. We have to leave.

A small backpack is suddenly in his hands.

KATIE: Hey, that's mine, how did you …?

TINO: We're running out of time.

KATIE: Stay away from me. I've called the police.

Panicking, KATIE *tries to get past him, but he blocks her path.*

TINO: I'm sorry but we have to leave right now. There is no option …

He extends his hand as if for her to take it, but instead she tries to pull him out of her way and moves to whack him on the head with the tablet. He expertly ducks out of the way, blows magic powder in her face and she instantly goes into a trance and follows him offstage.

SCENE NINE

PAUL *addresses the audience.*

PAUL: And then the pandemic struck. COVID-19. The twenty-first century plague. And everything changed.

Beat.

Everything stopped.

The world stood still.

And the environmental crisis was—by many—for a time forgotten.

The planes were grounded.

The cars mostly stayed parked.

Dolphins returned to canals in Venice. Perhaps. Or perhaps not …

In any case … People stayed home. Retreating to safety. In their ugg boots and dressing gowns, baking bread, tending to their gardens, watching Netflix, having Zoom cocktail parties and /

MADDY: [*offstage*] DAD! I need help with my maths worksheet!

PAUL: … Enduring home schooling /

MADDY: [*offstage*] What's an 'obtuse angle' mean?

PAUL: And maybe … Perhaps a part of me was a little relieved at hitting pause on the merry-go-round for a while. The idea of conservation, that's one thing—but active protest?

'To think is easy. To act is difficult. To act as one thinks is the most difficult.' That's Goethe.

Beat.

But really—I've always been more of a … 'Think globally, act locally, panic internally' sort of guy … A keyboard warrior at best until all this and then suddenly with Maddy …? Well—maybe what I'm saying is that lockdown seemed at first like a pretty useful circuit breaker.

Beat.

And for Maddy and I—saving the planet from impending environmental catastrophe? Maybe that might just have to wait a while.

News footage fills a screen. Emergency workers in face masks and shields. Centrelink queues. Shuttered shops. Empty city streets. Empty skies. Empty roads.

Music: something relevant, contemporary and with loads of energy, like 'The Kids are Coming', by Tones and I.

END OF ACT ONE

ACT TWO

SCENE ONE

KATIE *addresses the audience.*

KATIE: When I come to, I'm God knows where. And at my feet a backpack stuffed with … [*fumbling through it*] a towel … this strange tablet … and a couple of changes of undies.

TINO: Sorry.

KATIE: Rumbling through my underwear drawer … seriously … [*Realising something's missing. To* TINO] Hey, where's my phone? Where's my handbag?

TINO: Don't worry. I have it all under control. You'll soon be safe.

KATIE: Can you tell me where I am at least?

TINO: We had to get you out before the flights are grounded!

KATIE: Why are the planes going to be …? How do you know that …?

[*To the audience*] Suddenly I realise I'm seated in a small, too small, way too small, plane. Now rumbling down a tiny airstrip.

And we're off.

I look out the window hoping that someone might be speeding along the runway to rescue me but as the ground disappears from view below me, it hits me …

We're not in a Hollywood movie. I'm being kidnapped. And no-one is coming to rescue me. Career in ruin, a string of exes … No-one is coming, because no-one knows I'm gone. Because I've forgotten to keep any friends.

Who does that?

Alone.

And we fly low.

And I see the country.

The burnt-out veins of the land, still ashen from the fires.

And charred trees.

And dry rivers.

And I see.

And I see …

TINO: Time to wake up. We are here. We have arrived.
KATIE: Uh huh wha—?
TINO: Come on.

SCENE TWO

Paul and Maddy's home. They are at the dinner table.

PAUL: Hey, how was your day?
MADDY: Okay …
PAUL: Who did you hang out with at school?
MADDY: No-one really …
PAUL: No-one? Sounds fun.
Is everyone happy to be back and out of lockdown?
MADDY: Yeah, I suppose.
PAUL: Learn anything good then?
MADDY: Not really …

Pause.

PAUL: You're not eating.
MADDY: I'm not hungry.
PAUL: You've always loved spag bol.
MADDY: The meat, Dad. And the cheese. And there's egg in the pasta …
PAUL: Ah … Sorry.
MADDY: Dad—you know that going vegan can reduce our carbon footprint from food / by up to seventy-three per cent.
PAUL: By up to seventy-three per cent. Yes, sorry I do remember you learning that.

Beat.

I've got a lot on, Maddy. It's … stressful … at unI at the moment. Sorry, I'm not thinking properly. I'll make you something else. But you have to promise to eat it for me, okay?
MADDY: [*smiling, a little*] I'll think about it.
PAUL: Maddy, I don't want you to protest tomorrow. It's too dangerous now, I'm worried about you.

Pause.

[*Quietly but firmly*] Did you hear me? I don't want you to go this time.

Pause.

Well?

MADDY: I have to.

Pause.

Tomorrow is Friday. Hashtag Fridays for Future.

PAUL: You know it's illegal now, Maddy?

Pause.

[*Losing patience*] Are you listening to me? The current health orders don't allow it.

Pause.

[*Firmly*] I said no. You have to let it rest now for a bit.

A long silence.

MADDY: If I don't go, no-one will. You could come with me again if you're so worried? You haven't joined me in ages.

PAUL: I thought you didn't want me to come anymore?

MADDY: I didn't mean not ever … I'm just an eleven-year-old kid, Dad, what are they going to do? Arrest me?

PAUL *takes a long sigh.*

PAUL: Maddy. Maddy. Maddy.
Okay. But you have to at least wear your mask!

MADDY: I will, Dad, I will, I'll take care I promise.

PAUL: Okay. Now let me get you something to eat.

SCENE THREE

TINO *and* KATIE *drive in Samoa.* KATIE *addresses the audience.*

KATIE: And so I'm in this pickup truck now and we're dashing through narrow streets and busy markets, lots of stray dogs.

TINO: Get down!

KATIE: Past thatched huts and bungalows, past Eco-friendly resorts, past palm trees, many many many palm trees—and I'm struck by how lush and green it all is.

[*To* TINO] Where are we?

TINO: Malo. Welcome to Samoa! My home!

KATIE: Samoa! Why?

There's no response.

I'm quite hungry. Is there somewhere to—

TINO: Of course, of course! You must be starving! We will eat as soon as we arrive!

KATIE: [*to the audience*] And soon we found ourselves winding, up to the top of a mountain, shrouded in clouds. And as we wind higher and higher into the mist, although I was weak from hunger—I was a little glad not to have anything in my stomach …

[*To* TINO] Can we stop for a moment? I think I'm going to be /

TINO: Always look ahead—it will / help.

KATIE: How much higher up this mountain do we have to go?

TINO: This is no mountain. It's a volcano.

KATIE: What?

TINO: Don't worry. It's been a long time since it last erupted.

KATIE *is not comforted.*

KATIE: How long exactly?

TINO: [*passing her a paper bag*] Here—take this.

KATIE: [*to the audience*] I made it—just—without—you know—and—when we stop finally—breathtaking. We must be a thousand metres high up /

TINO: Yes, we're halfway. Welcome to Mount Silisili.

KATIE: We climb some steps around a steep cliff face until a strange little doorway appears before us. A doorway in the side of a rock face—high up in the clouds … what the /

TINO: Please come inside. [*In Samoan*] Sau ii. [*Wagging his fingers and pointing at her shoes*] Shoes!

She takes off her shoes. They walk inside.

SCENE FOUR

Outside the Courthouse, Wagga Wagga.

MADDY: Coal! Don't dig it! Leave it in the ground, it's time to get with it.

MADDY *repeats this. She encourages the audience to chant with her. A* POLICE OFFICER *appears behind her.*

POLICE OFFICER: Time to move on young lady.
MADDY: Thank you, I'm fine where I am, officer.
POLICE OFFICER: No you're not actually. Time to move on.
MADDY: I can't, I'm sorry.
POLICE OFFICER: This is not a legal march. You need to move on now.
MADDY: But I have a right to be here. It's a free country, isn't it?
POLICE OFFICER: There's a health order and this is the courthouse. You can't protest here.
MADDY: Then where can I protest?
POLICE OFFICER: Nowhere.
MADDY: Look—I'm even wearing my mask? See? [*More loudly*] 'COAL! DON'T DIG IT! LEAVE IT IN THE GROUND, IT'S TIME TO GET WITH IT!'
POLICE OFFICER: Help me out here. I'm not asking now, I'm telling. You have to leave. Who's here with you?
MADDY: It's just me …
POLICE OFFICER: Do your parents know you're here?
MADDY: Of course they do.
POLICE OFFICER: Then why / (aren't they here)?
MADDY: Because it's *my* future.
[*Even more loudly this time*] COAL! DON'T DIG IT! LEAVE IT IN THE / GROUND, IT'S TIME TO GET WITH IT!
POLICE OFFICER: Okay okay. Let's go now, you're coming with me, let's go!

The POLICE OFFICER *pulls* MADDY*'s hands behind her back and drags her.*

MADDY: What? What are you doing? Let go of me! Help! Let go of me!

The POLICE OFFICER *drags her offstage.*

SCENE FIVE

In Samoa, Tino's home. Inside the volcano.

KATIE: [*to the audience*] Inside now—and that innocuous doorway has revealed a sumptuous home in the side of this—hopefully dormant?—volcano. The room is warm, luxurious and strangely zen. Photos of generations of family adorning the walls … His family? If it is, his family goes back quite some way and includes a bird.

TINO *returns into the room, transformed to a suit of vibrant colour.*

[*To* TINO] Nice place … Nice outfit.

TINO: My family.

KATIE: And the bird?

TINO: The Manumea, Samoa's national bird.

My name is Tino Aviga Tamasese. Here—let me pour you some tea.

KATIE: For a moment we drink in silence and look out. The clouds have cleared and I see we are surrounded by rainforest. Far below—golden beaches, the ocean glistening in the sun. I hear the sound of bird calls just outside, and …

TINO: This is Shahin.

KATIE: [*trying to remain composed*] So are you going to tell me what I'm doing here now?

TINO: I have something for you. An important task. It's why I have brought you here.

KATIE: You mean dragged me here.

TINO: We were out of time. Now I know this will seem /

KATIE: You did say you had some food prepared?

TINO: Of course of course.

He claps his hands. Soup appears in front of her.

Soup! Bread!

KATIE: Wow.

TINO: This will likely sound /

KATIE: What if I asked for a gin and / tonic?

TINO: [*gesturing to her for quiet*] Please. By all means nourish yourself with this soup—you will need your energy.

KATIE: And why is that exactly …?

TINO: There is a job I need you to do. A package you must collect. It contains precious seeds that have been left for you and only you.

KATIE: Wait wait wait—you're not trying to get me to be some sort of drug mule for you? No no no no no, I'm not smuggling any 'package' for you and getting myself arrested in some foreign jail for the rest of my life. I'm not stupid—I've seen *Schapelle*. I've seen *Bangkok Hilton*.

TINO: [*laughing gently*] You misunderstand me. These are not drugs. These seeds will restore the ecological balance which has been so disrupted by / humanity.

KATIE: Sounds a lot like drugs to me …

TINO: Not drugs. Seeds.

KATIE: And they're what—magic or something? Like magic beans?

TINO: If you like.

KATIE: And you want me to … what exactly?

TINO: We will go together to collect them where they have been safely stored in anticipation of your arrival. And then you will plant them.

KATIE: [*laughing/spitting out her tea*] Okay you know I really think you may have kidnapped the wrong person here. It sounds like you're wanting me to be some sort of glorified courier—'bean' mule perhaps. Why on earth do you think I'm going to want to help you in this /

TINO: Because our world is dying. And we need you to help us save it.

SCENE SIX

Maddy and Paul's home.

PAUL: They've let you off. This time. With a warning. But this is serious, Maddy, you have to stop the protests. For good.

MADDY: Well that's not happening, is it.

PAUL: Maddy, we haven't got a choice. I've assured them you're done now.

MADDY: What? How am I done? Why would you say that?

PAUL: What did you expect? This time they've let you off. Next time I don't think we'll be so lucky.

MADDY: But we have to keep going. We're running out of time!

PAUL: For what? To save the world? Sweetheart, you have to stop.

MADDY: But we don't have time to stop! The Doomsday Clock is ticking! Scientists have just moved it to a hundred seconds to midnight. The closest it's ever been!

Pause.

PAUL: Maddy—this is not something we can just go and fix. It's too big!

MADDY: Whatever happened to 'Even the smallest person can change the course of the future'?

Pause.

PAUL *takes a deep breath.*

PAUL: [*smiling*] Okay. You're right.

Beat.

We can write letters together? Why don't we write to our local member again?

MADDY: Letters again? Seriously how old-school is that.

PAUL: We could start a petition?

MADDY *groans.*

How about a letter to the PM then?

MADDY *groans even louder.*

A really really good letter to the PM?

MADDY: I thought you wanted to do something real, Dad. I thought you were with me.

PAUL: I am with you, Maddy!

MADDY: No you're not. All you want to do is tell stories. Telling stories isn't actually DOING anything is it? Come with me to the next protest—like you used to.

PAUL: I can't Maddy. I could lose my job if I was even seen at one.

MADDY: You don't know that.

PAUL: I have a pretty good idea.

MADDY: Why did you tell me all about these heroes taking a risk to make a difference if you were too afraid to do it yourself then? Gandhi? Nelson Mandela? Rosa Parks? Did they save the world sitting on the sofa and tweeting?

PAUL: That's not fair, Maddy … I donate too!

MADDY: Being a keyboard warrior is not enough anymore, Dad. You have to stand up for what you believe in.
PAUL: I'm sorry. I really am. Maybe telling stories is all I have.

Beat.

This is not the time.

Beat.

You have to stop the Friday protests.

MADDY *leaves the room—furious.*

She sneaks out the back of the house, with a spray can in her hand.

SCENE SEVEN

In Samoa, Tino's home.

KATIE: I'm sorry? 'The planet is dying?' Oh no this isn't all about global warming, is it?
TINO: In our future—our current future—the Earth will die. Terrible overheating, famine, ice caps melting, sea levels rising. We haven't done enough. The governments of the world have not done enough.
KATIE: Look, I don't work for the government anymore. If this is part of some elaborate charade to get me to convince the minister about …
TINO: No, no. We have already long ago given up on the Australian Parliament. We've seen what happens when we wait for action.
KATIE: What do you mean, you've seen this already?
TINO: Eventually the governments of the world give up on our planet. The wreckage from human activity is just too great. Look out this window. All the houses, fishing boats, markets—and people—you saw as we arrived yesterday. They will all be swept away. Most of this island will be gone. Along with the homes of our brothers and sisters in Tuvalu, Laucala, Kiribati, Niue.
KATIE: Like Atlantis or something?
TINO: Exactly. Victims of humanity's obsession with more. But unlike Atlantis, our story is real.

Beat.

And so our children are sent away to find us a new home.

KATIE: A new island?

TINO: No—a new planet.

KATIE: Look this is all extremely fascinating but I'm not buying—Just take me back, okay?

SCENE EIGHT

Outside the police station. PAUL *paces and looks through photos on his phone. The* POLICE OFFICER *leads* MADDY *out. She bursts into tears as she runs to her father and hugs him.*

PAUL: Graffiti, Maddy? I don't believe this! Was this really *you*?

MADDY: You said I had to stop the Friday protests!

PAUL: But I didn't say you could start the Monday, Tuesday, Wednesday, Thursday, Saturday and Sunday protests! I didn't say you could graffiti! Maddy this is / (outrageous behaviour!)

MADDY: I thought people might see them along the river …

PAUL: Sneaking out in the dead of night, Maddy I don't believe it.

MADDY: Did you see them though?

PAUL: [*looking through photos taken of the graffiti*] 'Wake up humans, you're endangered too' … 'You Can't Recycle Wasted Time' … 'You'll die of old-age, I'll die of climate change' …

MADDY: Pretty good, hey?

PAUL: Those walls belong to people's businesses, Maddy. People's homes. They're not the ones responsible.

MADDY: Of course they are!

PAUL: What have they done to deserve this?

MADDY: They haven't done enough. No-one has. You said so yourself!

They leave the station.

PAUL: There are other problems in the world, now is not the time. I'm very disappointed in you, Madeleine.

MADDY: You're just like all the politicians now, aren't you. 'Now is not the time.'

PAUL: Just because it doesn't happen now, doesn't mean it won't ever happen.

MADDY: You don't know that. If we just go back to shouting at the news nothing will change.

PAUL: Some people won't change their way of life without a fight, Maddy. Change is hard.

MADDY: So—what—we're supposed to just give up? Sit on our hands and wait?

PAUL: Even if you and all your friends protested every single day, even if you managed to organise a thousand students to walk from here to Canberra and protest outside Parliament House—it won't be …

MADDY: Say that again?

PAUL: I said even if you organised a thousand students to walk from here to / Canberra …

MADDY: To Canberra. A student walk to Canberra. That's brilliant, Daddy. That's genius.

PAUL: But I / didn't …

MADDY: Thank you. Thank you. I love you, Daddy. That's brilliant.

She throws her arms around him.

PAUL: [*to himself*] Why do I keep talking? Why do I even open my mouth?

SCENE NINE

In Samoa, Tino's home.

TINO: [*blocking* KATIE*'s exit*] You cannot leave. We need you. And we are out of time.

KATIE: Oh please come on … [*Trying to get past him*] There's always more time.

TINO: [*still blocking her path*] Yes, that is what we all thought. What we all said. But we were kidding ourselves. It's already happening. Right here, right now, our lives are changing forever. And it doesn't get any better.

KATIE: How do you know?

TINO: Because I look at the sky and I look at the ocean, and I can see the change to my home. Every day. Every week.

KATIE: But—

TINO: Because I've seen the future.

KATIE: What?

TINO: And because I've met your daughter.

KATIE: My daughter? I don't have a /

TINO: You will one day. Her name is Ava, she's a biologist and she was part of a mission …

KATIE: Ava …

KATIE *'s impressed.*

A biologist, huh. So who's the kid's father? A doctor? Lawyer? Dentist?

TINO: This is not important / what is …

KATIE: It is to / me!

TINO: Your daughter was one of the children sent away to find somewhere else for us all to live. And when she came back, she had discovered more than just a new home. She returned with a solution.

KATIE: And this is what you want me to pick up and smuggle across borders around the world.

TINO: Well I wouldn't have said smuggle …

KATIE: Where did they come from?

TINO: From Planet B.

KATIE: Okay now I know you're taking the /

KATIE *bursts out laughing.*

TINO: It's not officially Planet B of course. Kepler Four Five Two B is its real / name.

KATIE: [*still laughing*] Kepler Four Five … what? Like the potato?

TINO: It's several galaxies away orbiting a red dwarf star.

KATIE: [*laughing uncontrollably*] And you're trying to tell me my daughter travels back from potato planet all she wants to give me is a bunch of / seeds.

TINO: We've been trying to get in touch with you for some time you know.

KATIE: [*sarcastically*] What? How?

TINO: Those letters.

KATIE *stops laughing.*

I understand this is a lot to take in. But Ava is counting on you.

SCENE TEN

Somewhere in Canberra ... Sounds of music, drums, chanting ...

MADDY *has a drum. She addresses the crowd with a loudhailer.*

MADDY: The youth. Are rising. No more compromising.

She repeats this and leads the crowd in the chant.

Today, you have all done something amazing! Everyone said we couldn't do this!

We've come here from all over the state to make our voices heard.

We did it!

But before we reach Parliament House, I want us all to remember, they will be waiting for us.

'Dark and difficult times lie ahead. Soon we must face a choice between what is right and what is easy!' Dumbledore.

But this is no fantasy. This is our planet! And it's really happening! It is our lives they're playing with. And we need the federal government to stop digging up our future. We need them to listen to the science and see that our world is *literally* on fire.

We're a small country but currently we are leading the way in destroying the planet.

There is no Planet B. So we need a *Plan* B.

We have all been betrayed. By our parents, and our grandparents. They made us think that ditching plastic straws, recycling and having shorter showers would make it all go away. But it's not even close to enough! They ignored this crisis for too long. And now they've left it up to us. Well we won't sit on our hands and wait for someone else to rescue us. We are going to strike. And we're going to keep striking until those with the power to do something start acting like their lives depended on it.

We may be small in numbers. We may not yet be old enough to vote. But we *can* make a difference.

Repeat after me! What do we want? CLIMATE ACTION! When do we want it? NOW!

She encourages the audience to join in the chant.

Music. Drums. Cheering.

SCENE ELEVEN

This scene splits between KATIE *and* TINO *in Tino's home and* PAUL *and* MADDY *at a youth detention centre.*

In Samoa

KATIE: And when do we have to do this thing?
TINO: Now. We have to leave right now. All the seeds must be planted before the next total lunar eclipse It's just a week away.
KATIE: No pressure, right?

MADDY *and* PAUL *sit across from each other at a table—a meeting room in a youth detention centre.*

PAUL: Are they feeding you okay?
MADDY: [*flatly*] It's okay.
PAUL: Really?
MADDY: No, it's pretty gross.
PAUL: So are you eating then or not?
MADDY: 'You eat what you get and don't get upset.'
PAUL: Maddy, you have to / eat.
MADDY: [*flatly*] It's fine, Dad.
PAUL: Youth detention is not fine, Maddy. [*His temper flaring*] I can't believe …

Tino's home.

KATIE: So where exactly do you want to take me?
TINO: Svalbard. The seeds are waiting for us there.
KATIE: Skal-hard?
TINO: Svalbard. Part of Norway. To the Doomsday Vault.
KATIE: The what?

The detention centre.

PAUL: You told me you were going away with your mother!

Pause.

Uh-huh. Exactly.

MADDY: … I'm sorry.
PAUL: Maddy, you can't save the world in a week.
MADDY: At least I tried.
PAUL: And you also can't save the world if you get yourself killed.
MADDY: … Wow …

Tino's home.

KATIE: Why the grim name?
TINO: The vault stores essential seeds there in case /
KATIE: Doomsday comes.
TINO: Precisely.
KATIE: And seeds are the things that will save us?

The detention centre.

PAUL: Tell me more about what actually happened …
MADDY: [*brightening a little*] Well first we caught the bus to Gundagai.
PAUL: [*singing*] 'There's a track winding back … '
MADDY: And then by the time we got to Canberra. There were thousands. Thousands!
PAUL: And the police were there to meet you.
MADDY: They had this capsicum spray. And this armour …like Storm Troopers.
PAUL: Not the prime minister.
MADDY: Definitely not.
PAUL: Or the environment minister?
MADDY: [*shaking her head*] Lots of TV cameras, but.
PAUL: So whose idea was it to chain yourselves to the flagpole? Was it your idea?
MADDY: Sort of. Not just me …

Pause.

PAUL: I heard your speech.

Pause.

It was a pretty great speech.

Pause.

MADDY: I just want to go home.

They reach out to each other across the table and grip each other's hands as tightly as they possibly can.

Tino's home.

TINO: So will you do it?

KATIE: Do I have a choice?

TINO: Not really. The planet is counting on you, Miss Katie.

A long moment.

KATIE: Doomsday here we come!

TINO: Good choice. Shahin!

He claps his hands.

KATIE: What—wait—is the bird coming too?

And the falcon SHAHIN *flies to land on* TINO*'s arm.*

Music: a song should play here, again relevant and contemporary please. Ideally, 'The Doomsday Clock', by Abbe May.

END OF ACT TWO

ACT THREE

SCENE ONE

PAUL *and* KATIE *address the audience.*

PAUL: Once upon a time there was a young princess who was very very spoiled and very very selfish. One day when she was playing by the pond, she heard a frog croaking. He seemed to be caught on some weeds in the pond, or maybe it was a plastic ring. It was a southern corroboree frog. Which is endangered.

KATIE: The girl didn't know this. And she ignored it.

PAUL: She didn't know he was one of the last of his kind and if she didn't save him, the whole species may very well become extinct. When the frog croaked at the girl, she pretended not to hear it at all.

KATIE: She was too busy playing. She had a beautiful golden ball. It was her favourite toy.

PAUL: And she had a lot of amazing toys, so that was saying something. Maybe it was the way the light caught the golden ball.

KATIE: Or maybe it was that beautiful little tinkling sound as she rolled it or threw it into the air.

PAUL: But today, when she threw it into the air—it landed in the pond.

KATIE: And she hated the pond. She couldn't stand the smell. It made her want to be sick. She called out for her mother, the Queen, to come and fetch her ball for her. But no answer. She called out for her father the King to come and fetch her ball for her. But no answer. She called for a servant! She even whistled for her dog. But no-one came.

Then there was a sound. From the pond itself.

PAUL: 'Excuse me! Would you like me to fetch your ball for you? I could help you if you like?'

KATIE: [*deeply suspicious*] 'Really? Is this a trick?'

PAUL: 'No trick. You just have to help me untangle myself from the reeds—and this plastic ring. I've been croaking for help but I seem to be all alone here.'

KATIE: The selfish young princess nearly felt sorry for the frog. Perhaps because she also felt a certain kinship. She also felt alone.

'But the reeds are so smelly. And dirty. And I never go anywhere near the pond.'

PAUL: What to do? To save her ball, and so she could keep playing her game, she would have to help the frog.

KATIE: But to help, she would have to overcome her deep aversion to the slimy frog, and, let's be honest, her deep aversion generally to helping others.

PAUL: 'Please help me. It's getting warmer in this water every day and I really need to get free. I promise as soon as I'm loose I'll fetch your beautiful ball.'

KATIE: What to do?

MADDY *is revealed.* PAUL *has been telling her a story. It's a flashback to when* MADDY *was much younger.*

PAUL: But without this simple act of kindness, Maddy, the frog couldn't save the princess.

MADDY: But the princess could save the frog.

PAUL: Exactly. Time for sleep now, my sweetheart.

[*To the audience*] When she was arrested, Maddy was handcuffed, searched, dragged to a police station, interviewed for hours. And because it was a weekend, she was held 'in custody' until the hearing.

No-one reading stories at night to kids in jail.

MADDY: Stuck in a detention centre, in a bare room, with a scungy old mattress on a hard steel bed ... I thought school camp was hard.

Beat.

And who knew I could actually be arrested! I'm twelve!

PAUL: The age of criminal responsibility in most of Australia now—it's just ten years old.

MADDY: At ten, you were still reading me bedtime stories. At ten, you barely let me out of the house by myself. At ten, you wouldn't even let me watch the last two Harry Potter films!

PAUL: Maybe I should have protected you more. Let you stay a kid longer.

MADDY: Too late for that.

PAUL: After an agonising wait, she was finally released on bail.

MADDY: Home again.

Beat.

This is my story now.

SCENE TWO

In Svalbard.

KATIE: All I can see is snow, Tino. Snow, snow, snow in every direction! Where are we headed? Why all the way out here?
TINO: It's freezing. It's isolated. Do you see anyone else here?
KATIE: Not a living soul.

The Doomsday Vault, Svalbard.

The hard steel doors of the vault open and an elderly Norwegian woman, SOLVEIG, *approaches them.*

SOLVEIG: Hei. Hei. (Hi.)
God Kveld. (Good evening.)
Hvordan goaar det med deg? (How are you?)
TINO: It's me, Tino.
SOLVEIG: Tino! Lenge siden sist. (Long time no see.)

SOLVEIG *and* TINO *embrace.* SOLVEIG *then turns to* KATIE.

[*Suddenly beaming at them both*] Welcome! Welcome! Welcome! At long last. It's so good to meet you, Miss Petersen. /
KATIE: Katie is fine—how did you /
SOLVEIG: My name is Solveig. Welcome to the Svalbard Global Seed Vault!

SOLVEIG *leads them inside through the grand entrance of the seed vault.*

Come, come inside and see. Come and see what we have been holding for you all these years.

SOLVEIG *takes out a box that appears to be wrapped in an old tea towel. Then from inside reveals inside, three tightly woven bags of gleaming crystals.*

TINO: Incredible.
KATIE: They're gleaming! Are they the …

They each open a bag and examine its contents.

TINO: Shimmering gold.
KATIE: Arctic blue.
SOLVEIG: And glittering emerald green.
KATIE: These are exquisite! They are all—for us?
SOLVEIG: She also left you a gift

She hands KATIE *a jewelled necklace also wrapped in the towel.*

KATIE: So …[*Holding it*] heavy! I love it. Where's it from?
SOLVEIG: Kepler B.

KATIE *nearly drops the necklace.*

And a note too—here.
KATIE: [*Reading*] 'I want to see the world the way you saw it. Let's change history together. Ava.'
SOLVEIG: Wonderful, no? You know what to do then?
KATIE: [*overwhelmed*] Well …I don't. I mean. Sort of? But not exactly.

SOLVEIG *clears her throat.*

SOLVEIG: [*briskly*] You have here seven seeds you need to plant across the globe. You must plant each and every single little one of them. Remember there are no spares. The *green* are to be planted deep into the soil, in our largest continents. The *gold* are to be buried in the sand, in our vast deserts. Lastly, the *blue* seeds must be planted in our two greatest oceans—buried deep within the ocean floor. You understand?
KATIE: I—I—I—continents …deserts …oceans.

She reaches for support.

Tino—help?
TINO: [*soothing*] You'll be fine, Katie.
[*To* SOLVEIG] We will do what needs to be done.
SOLVEIG: [*quietly to* TINO] Are you sure she can do this?
TINO: [*quietly*] She would not have been chosen otherwise.
SOLVEIG: [*raising one eyebrow*] By her own daughter?
TINO: She must have given her cause to trust her. And so we must also.
SOLVEIG: Must we now?

Pause.

I'm sorry I'm not convinced.

TINO: What are you suggesting?

SOLVEIG: I'm not releasing these seeds for just anyone. There are no second chances with this task. And this …girl …

TINO: It's less than a week until the eclipse.

SOLVEIG: Until you give me a reason to trust her—the seeds stay with me.

She walks away. TINO *returns to* KATIE.

KATIE: What? What did she /

TINO: Everything is fine.

KATIE: Then why is she leaving with our seeds?

SCENE THREE

Maddy and Paul's home.

PAUL: Maddy, you know you're only out on bail on condition that you don't protest anywhere, or see any of the people who joined you on the march.

MADDY: Seriously? That is ALL my friends. How is that even possible?

PAUL: The court case will come around before we know it. So you have to keep a low profile from now on, okay? No more Fridays for Future protests. And definitely no sneaking out at night. Do you promise?

MADDY: [*very reluctantly*] … Okay …

PAUL: [*a little pleasantly surprised*] Good.

MADDY: Hashtag Fridays for Future is on temporary break.

PAUL: [*a bit more sceptically*] Thank you …
Now let's lawyer up!

MADDY: [*to the audience*] Finding a lawyer turned out to be harder than we thought. I mean we got A LOT of calls, but /

PAUL: We need to find someone who understands you, Maddy.

The screen lights up with ADRIAN *on a Zoom call.*

ADRIAN: [*on the screen*] So in my opinion we are on very strong ground in defending the case against you. I would argue it's your constitutional right to protest and that you were acting in self-defence to protect your future. I think we can make sure you leave the Children's Court with nothing more than a caution.

PAUL: But what about the flagpole business?

ADRIAN: Well yes—they've called that 'obstructing traffic' because you were blocking the entrance to Parliament House. I mean it's definitely serious, but I do think we can get all these offences dismissed by a magistrate, since they were all part of the same protest action.

MADDY: Excellent!

ADRIAN: But we have a much bigger opportunity here. You're big news right now, Maddy. I think we can really use this attention to our advantage. What do you want more than anything right now?

MADDY: I want the government to do something!

ADRIAN: Well, how about we make them? Through the courts. How would you like to sue the Minister for the Environment?

PAUL: What? What would *we* be suing anyone for?

MADDY: Dad—stop interrupting I want to / hear what …

PAUL: Maddy …

ADRIAN: The way I see it, the government has breached its duty of care to you. It's avoided its responsibility for far too long. You're paying for it now. And you will be paying for it in the future.

Beat.

It's simple negligence law.

MADDY: Are you serious? I can sue the government?

PAUL: Maddy, we might discuss this—just the two of us?

MADDY: Mr …

ADRIAN: Call me Adrian—

MADDY: Won't this be /

ADRIAN: Expensive? Don't worry about that—I'll do it pro bono.

MADDY: Pro what?

ADRIAN: Free.

PAUL: Maddy … later /

MADDY: Dad, this sounds / amazing.

ADRIAN: You should know that if we do this, Maddy, we would need to have an adult's name on the case as well as yours. So you do both really need to be on board.

PAUL: Thank you for your time, Adrian.

PAUL *turns off the screen.*

MADDY: Dad—why did you send him away? He's the one.

PAUL: It's *insane*, Maddy. It's just asking for trouble. What we need to focus on is clearing these charges against you.

MADDY: No no no no no, you have to get him back. You have to get him back.

PAUL: But to do what he's suggesting. It could take years. And an army of very expensive lawyers. We don't have either.

MADDY: But he said it would be free.

PAUL Nothing is ever free.

MADDY: Can't we at least try?

PAUL: If my name is on the case too, Maddy … I really don't know how the university is going to react. It's so risky.

MADDY: Can't you at least ask?

PAUL: The government will hit back so hard …

> MADDY *mouths 'Please.'*

> PAUL *laughs gently, kisses her on the head and leaves the room.*

SCENE FOUR

This scene splits between MADDY *and* PAUL *at their home and* KATIE *and* TINO *in Svalbard.*

KATIE *and* TINO *are outside the Doomsday Vault.*

TINO: Are you ready to do this, Miss Katie? Can we count on you?

KATIE: But how can I get right around the world in less than a week and /

TINO: Quickly!

KATIE: Thanks a lot.

> TINO *claps his hands loudly and* SHAHIN *arrives and lands on his arm.*

TINO: Shahin is a peregrine falcon—the fastest animal on Earth. He can travel nearly four hundred kilometres an hour.

KATIE: And what, I'm flying with the bird?

TINO: You must find the source of your strength, and channel it now for this cause. Look deep inside yourself. Look, Miss Katie … Are you looking?

KATIE: Yes!

TINO: And what do you see?
KATIE: I—I—I don't see anything!

Beat.

I'm sorry Tino. I just can't. You have the wrong person.

KATIE *runs through the snow. And she runs and runs and runs.*

TINO: Shahin—follow her!

The falcon flies after her.

Maddy and Paul's home. MADDY *and* PAUL *both bring onstage countless very large, very heavy legal texts.*

MADDY *addresses the audience.*

MADDY: So Dad finally gave in and gave Adrian a chance. But he didn't get an army of lawyers with him. It was just the one. Just him.
PAUL: The government is going to come at us armed with way more resources, more experience, more money /
MADDY: And way more lawyers.
PAUL: I'm going to have to come on board to help Adrian with research. Looks like I'll have to take some time off work.
MADDY: So do I get to take time off school too then?
PAUL: Not a chance.
MADDY: [*to the audience*] Dad crams all this case law and picks up all these old legal textbooks and old news stories and does what he can to help Adrian prepare his arguments. And I do what I can too—before and after school—courtesy of Google.

Svalbard. KATIE *finally stops running to catch her breath, she looks around her in all directions.*

KATIE: [*to herself*] Where on Earth am I? [*Spotting something in the distance ahead of her*] Is that another polar bear out there …? It looks stranded. The ice has melted all around her. [*Calling out*] Hello?! Is anyone … [*She suddenly clutches her chest*] I'm going to be …

Suddenly there is a noise from behind her, and another POLAR BEAR *appears over the horizon and starts moving towards her.*

[*Quietly*] Another one? Oh boy oh boy oh boy oh boy …

The POLAR BEAR *keeps up its pace pounding the snow, heaving its great body towards her.* SHAHIN *appears above and watches. But the* POLAR BEAR *keeps moving.*

[*To herself*] Stay calm, stay calm … Do I take the melting ice cap polar bear or the one right behind me?

SHAHIN *comes to rest on* KATIE*'s shoulder. The* POLAR BEAR *approaches and rests at her feet.*

What the—? [*Whispering to the bird*] What do I do, Shahin?

SHAHIN *jumps onto the* POLAR BEAR*'s back.*

What the heck. What have I got to lose?

She climbs onto the POLAR BEAR*'s back and throws her arms around its neck. The* POLAR BEAR *stands up and begins to move.*

Woah! Take it easy there, I've never done this before!

TINO *is out looking for* KATIE.

TINO: KATIE! KATIE!

SOLVEIG: [*joining him*] Where on Earth did she run to?

KATIE *now appears triumphantly on the back of the* POLAR BEAR, *with* SHAHIN *flying above her head.* TINO *rushes to her and helps her dismount.*

KATIE: Tino, Solveig … This incredible creature took me right to the edge of our collapsing world. I can't unsee it. I can't look away any longer.

TINO: [*beaming and leading her by the hand to* SOLVEIG] With Shahin to guide her, she can do this. Now please—you have to trust us.

KATIE: No-one has ever chosen me for anything before. When I was a kid, I was never chosen for the netball team. I've never even been chosen for jury duty! But there's always a first.

[*To* SOLVEIG] I promise you. I won't let you down.

SOLVEIG: You had better not. You go girl!

She gives KATIE *the seeds, still carefully wrapped.*

TINO: [*handing* KATIE *a small jar*] You'll also need these when you are planting the blue seeds.

KATIE: Yeeewww—they look like slugs.

TINO: They are.

KATIE: [*holding back her revulsion and quickly putting the jar in her backpack*] Okay … What do I—

TINO: Grab hold of Shahin and go like the wind!

SOLVEIG: Good luck!

TINO *blows magic powder at* SHAHIN. *Who suddenly grows. And grows. And grows.*

Maddy and Paul's home.

PAUL: [*slamming his laptop shut, standing up, exclaiming*] Gah!

MADDY: What's wrong, Dad?

PAUL: It's just all so infuriating!

MADDY: What?

PAUL: That we have to argue this case to the courts and to the government. When they already know it all. Here—there's this intergovernmental panel on climate change with leading scientists spelling it all out—it's from 1988! Here's a greenhouse conference in Australia—1987. Reports from the CSIRO—1971! And look at this one—this tiny news story here—four lines—here in July 1912, in a local newspaper in Braidwood—a mining town just a few hours from here, warning that burning coal was likely to be a bad idea. 1912. That's nearly one hundred and ten years ago.

MADDY: So what did they do?

PAUL: Nothing. The story vanished.

MADDY: But the government knew?

PAUL: Absolutely. Look—more and more reports. From ASIO, from the CSIRO, they have it all, they knew it all. Predictions of fires, of floods, of the impact on our rivers, even of pandemics. And what did they do? Bury the findings and dig another coal mine. And fossil fuel companies—there's all these internal memos going all the way back to the sixties! They've all known for decades. And yet they've kept polluting all this time. It's like big tobacco all over again.

MADDY *walks over to him.*

MADDY: [*taking his hand*] Maybe you need to take a break now, Dad. Shouldn't you be at uni, anyway?

PAUL: I've got someone covering for me. We've got to keep going. Your Doomsday Clock is still ticking.

Somewhere above Svalbard, SHAHIN *has picked* KATIE *up and they both fly high in the sky together.*

KATIE: Yeeeeaahhhh! Incredible! I'm flyyyyyiiiiinnnnggggg!
So Shahin I assume you know where we're going?

SHAHIN *nods in response.*

That's lucky—for both of us.

Beat.

Look at all the birds flying with us! Are they following us? Or are we following them? Hey, Shahin, what if we see a plane?

SHAHIN *ducks down, and then returns.*

We duck? That's your answer? Let's hope most of the flights are still grounded!

SHAHIN *and* KATIE *land.*

These fields look pretty empty to me. How are we supposed to know where to go?

SHAHIN *taps her bag and the tablet falls out.*

The GPS. Right. Got it. [*Studying the map*] Siberia? We're in Siberia?

She walks a few paces and the tablet lights up.

Okay, so I'm guessing it's here. Let's bury our treasure deep in the earth. The first of the green seeds. [*Tapping the hard earth*] I don't suppose you brought a shovel?

SHAHIN *helps her dig a hole deep in the earth, and* KATIE *plants the first green seed ... Nothing happens.*

Well that's a little bit anti-climactic, isn't it! Am I supposed to water it or something?

They sit together and eat some of their supplies. Behind them, through the trees, we hear, then we see, a SIBERIAN TIGER *emerge.*

[*Whispering*] Is that a Siberian tiger?

The SIBERIAN TIGER *comes right up to them and bows her head momentarily. Then sits exactly where the seeds were planted and rests there.*

[*Quietly*] What's she doing? Is she … is she … guarding the seeds?

SCENE SIX

SHAHIN *and* KATIE *are flying again.*

KATIE: Shahin—the map's telling me our next stop is the Congo—Odzala-Kokoua National Park! Do you know how to get there?

SHAHIN *nods—and indicates straight ahead. They continue to fly, then start to descend.*

Oh look down there, that must be it! Lush, green forests, and look at that powerful winding river. Pinch me now!

They land on the ground.

What a view, Shahin! We're surrounded by stunning old rainforests! Breathe in that beautiful fresh air! Fill your lungs with it!

Beat.

Let's dig this one nice and deep.

They do, and as they finish planting the seed, there's a noise in front of them, and an imposing shape approaches. KATIE *gently backs away.*

[*To herself*] No fast movements—gently, gently—smile at the nice gorilla!

The GORILLA *moves to where the seed was planted, bows his head towards them, and stands guard.*

So this is where we plant our second green seed.
Now what? Cocoa break?

SHAHIN *nudges her up to her feet.*

Okay okay, time to get moving again is it? Well then let's go!
Keep that seed safe. See you later, Gorilla, okay? Just a bit amazing!

SCENE SEVEN

This scene splits between MADDY *and* PAUL *and* KATIE *and* SHAHIN *on their quest.*

MADDY *and* PAUL *lie on top of their car, looking up at the stars.* PAUL *is wearing a T-shirt that reads 'My child is revolting. #ProudDad'.*

MADDY: Do you think there's another planet out there, Dad? You know—if we don't find a solution for this one?

PAUL: Oooh—how about that one there? Do you reckon that one would work?

MADDY: What? Which one? Where?

PAUL: See the three stars in a row there in the middle of that constellation … up there … no straight up there … Got it?

MADDY: Maybe?

PAUL: That constellation is known as Orion the Hunter, and those three stars—they're Orion's Belt.

MADDY: Okay …?

PAUL: Now follow up and—do you see that bright star on the left? That one in Orion's armpit …

MADDY: Gross … Oh that reddish dot there?

PAUL: Exactly. It's called Betelgeuse.

MADDY: Beetlejuice? Like that old movie?

PAUL: [*laughing*] Well—maybe! It's also near where Ford Prefect is supposed to come from in *The Hitchhiker's Guide to the Galaxy*.

MADDY: Seriously? That old book again.

PAUL: Ha—*The Planet of the Apes* was also set on a planet circling Betelgeuse!

MADDY: So what's so special about it then?

PAUL: I really don't know. And—well—most of the stars out there could have planets circling them, just like we circle the sun, but it's those bright red giant stars that people think are the most likely options to have *habitable* planets around them.

MADDY: You mean planets where we could live.

PAUL: Exactly … And that's a pretty bright star—so who knows—maybe …

MADDY: And how long would it take to get there.

PAUL: A lifetime. Several really. If we even could.
MADDY: Ah.
PAUL: The truth is none of us know …
MADDY: Let's stick with Planet Earth?
PAUL: You betcha …
MADDY: Dad are you ever going back to teach?
PAUL: It's hard at the moment … There've been some cutbacks …
MADDY: Not you?

PAUL nods.

Oh Dad I'm sorry.

PAUL: It's not your fault … Come on … how about another hot choccy? We've got another couple of hours' drive ahead of us tomorrow.

KATIE and SHAHIN are flying again.

KATIE: So once we cross the Red Sea, Shahin, next stop is the Arabian Desert!

Look at those rolling golden sands stretching out below us …

They land and dig the next seed deep into the sandy plains. Again a sound is heard. From one side, then from the other, two sets of eyes peer over a sand dune. Two SAND GAZELLES emerge.

Two gorgeously graceful sand gazelles. Keep a good lookout, you two! Thanks for watching over our seedling!

SCENE EIGHT

This scene splits between MADDY and PAUL in court and KATIE and SHAHIN on their quest.

Outside the Children's Court of New South Wales in Sydney. MADDY addresses the audience.

MADDY: So we've just spent the day in court, at the Children's Court of New South Wales. I dressed up for the occasion—Dad insisted.
ADRIAN: I think that all went pretty well, don't you?
PAUL: What, except for when they accused me of child neglect.
MADDY: Or called me a delinquent troublemaker.
ADRIAN: Other than that! I think we managed to keep to the point—which is your right to protest and protect your future, even during a pandemic.

PAUL: So what happens now?

ADRIAN: Well that's just part one. It's with the magistrate for now. Part two is the Supreme Court for the 'big one'.

MADDY: Maddy versus the Minister.

ADRIAN: That's the one. Feeling ready?

MADDY: Ready as I'll ever be.

ADRIAN: That's the way. Now I've got to go to Melbourne tomorrow to meet with another client. Enjoy your day off.

KATIE *and* SHAHIN *land in Australia.*

KATIE: Well, Shahin, we're back home in Oz. The Great Munga-Thirri-Simpson Desert in the red centre. Our second golden seed. Onya little seed. Make some magic for us!

They stand back to see who comes to guard their treasure, and a BILBY, *a* ROCK WALLABY *and a* PINK COCKATOO *emerge.*

A bilby, a rock wallaby and a pink cockatoo.

She salutes the wildlife trio.

Keep an eye on her for me, fellas!

SHAHIN *scoops* KATIE *up.*

Can't we stay a bit longer?

SHAHIN *shakes his head and they fly off again.*

No time to lose, hey.

Beat.

SHAHIN *yawns.*

[*Checking her tablet*] Where in the world is Patagonia?

Outside the Supreme Court of New South Wales.

ADRIAN: [*speaking over Zoom on Paul's phone*] How are you feeling, Maddy?

MADDY: Pretty nervous.

ADRIAN: You'll be great. I'm really sorry I can't get back to Sydney in time now. Melbourne's just gone back into lockdown overnight. But—I'll be right there right beside you—virtually.

MADDY: Can't they just wait until you can be here in person?

ADRIAN: I've asked, filed a motion for a stay of proceedings, but the government has denied it. Your dad has got all my notes with him just in case there's any hiccups.

PAUL: Looks like you've got quite the storm coming your way too, Adrian.

ADRIAN: Once in a hundred year storm they say. Lucky you both missed it on your drive up to Sydney! I'll be okay. This old house isn't going anywhere.

PAUL: Stay safe. See you in court!

ADRIAN: See you in court!

KATIE *and* SHAHIN *are flying.*

KATIE: Come on, Shahin, I know you can do it. I know you're tired, and if I could just do it without you I would but … we really don't have time for too many more breaks and just please please please don't drop me on top of one of these snow-capped mountains.

SHAHIN *grunts and nods.*

I am! I'm holding on as tight as I can, I swear!

In court. ADRIAN *is videoconferencing in.*

ADRIAN: Your honour. My client argues that the Australian government has been negligent in refusing to mitigate the risks of major and long-lived social and health impacts of climate change.

Sounds of heavy storms in the background, they become louder.

That despite repeated scientific warnings and evidence over many decades, the government has chosen at best inaction—

A lightning flash, and thunder follows shortly after. The image breaks up.

… And at worst taken a course that increases the risk posed to my client, and jeopardises the security of her whole—

The image breaks up again as a loud thunderclap interrupts him.

… Generation.

The video cuts out altogether. There's just the sound of static and flashes across the screen.

MADDY: Where did he go? Is he coming back? Is he okay?

MADDY *addresses the audience.*

People were trying to adjust the screen, the computer controls, trying to call Adrian on their phones.

PAUL *returns.*

[*To* PAUL] What's happening?

PAUL: We're having a short recess and if we can't get Adrian back, it looks like I'm going to have to continue with his opening statement …

MADDY: You? But you're not a lawyer!

SHAHIN *and* KATIE *land in the Patagonian Desert.*

KATIE: You made it! Woo-hoo! [*Hugging* SHAHIN] You're incredible. Okay let's find out where our seed needs to find its home.

SHAHIN *nods his head down towards another part of the desert.*

Down here you think? Careful it's rocky here and so dry, do you need me to carry you? [*Checking her GPS on her tablet*] It's here. Let's bury our final golden seed. In this barren desert.

There's a sound. Footsteps.

What's that?

They both lie flat in an attempt not to be seen.

You know, Shahin, I feel like David Attenborough here. [*Attempting to mimic his distinctive voice*] 'Here in the Patagonian Desert, an Andean deer appears and surveys the arid landscape around it. It comes to a rocky outcrop and searches for prey. The deer stands guard.'

In the court, the screen is still static. No sign of ADRIAN.

PAUL: Maddy, I'm not sure I can do this.

MADDY: Dad—just read the notes. You'll be fine. Pretend you're in a lecture.

PAUL: I'm not as brave as you, Maddy.

MADDY: You can do it, Dad, I know you can. Just tell them our story.

PAUL: You said my stories weren't enough anymore.

MADDY: They've gotten us this far, haven't they? You're the one who inspired me to do all this. Inspire them too. 'Unless someone like you cares a whole awful lot ...'

PAUL: 'Nothing is going to get better. It's not'

Somewhere in the Patagonian Desert. KATIE *and* SHAHIN *eat together.*

KATIE: So Shahin—we still have two blue seeds left. Do I just drop them in the ocean as we pass over?

SHAHIN *nudges the backpack and the jar falls out.*

The slugs. How could I forget ... [*Sticking them in her ears*] Gross! But also ... [*puzzled*] ... warming? What are they supposed to be for?

SHAHIN *breathes deeply.*

Oh—breathing underwater. Okay helpful then! To the Pacific. Let's dive on in!

In court. PAUL *picks up his notes, nervously, stands and begins reading.*

PAUL: Thank you for your patience, your honour. To continue where my colleague left off ... The government ... has a clear and direct duty of care ... to my ... client ...

MADDY: [*whispering*] Keep going, Dad.

PAUL: ... And not only to my client but to all young Australians ... And that duty has been breached.

PAUL *puts down his notes.*

Your honour, my daughter is a young citizen of Australia, born in this country. She plans to have children and grandchildren here, in her hometown of Wagga Wagga, to work and build a family here. Isn't it the government's prime responsibility to protect its citizens? Shouldn't I—as her father—be able to expect that if my government knew of major risks to her safety—to her future that they will act on that knowledge?

In the news today. We have wild storms in Melbourne, mass flooding around the state.

This is what climate change looks like. We're not talking about something coming for us in the future. We're already here. Our planet is already one point two degrees hotter than before the industrial revolution.

The government will argue that we are a small country. That what we do can't make a difference. But if even the smallest person [*indicating* MADDY] can change our town, so too a small country can change the world.

Now my local community. It's doing what it can. But is the federal government?

They've seen the data. They have the power to do something. To set policy. To take action. But they have done nothing.

We all know of the perils of climate change. My daughter, a twelve-year-old girl, knows that the clock is ticking.

So if everyone knows—then isn't the failure to act—effectively throwing an entire generation under the bus—well if that's not negligence, I don't know what is.

And people wonder why my daughter is protesting.

The wonder should be why she wouldn't.

On an island somewhere in the Pacific.

KATIE: [*coughing up sea water*] Are you KIDDING me? I am not doing that again. Take me back. Take me home NOW. I am done. We've planted two green seeds in the earth, three golden ones in the desert, and God knows if they'll actually do anything. You could have killed me back there! One blue seed in the Pacific Ocean floor—that's going to have to be enough …

Silence.

Say something you … you overgrown Big Bird!

SHAHIN *nudges her backpack again. A towel falls out. She starts to dry herself and* SHAHIN. *The sun starts to rise. And they sit there, on a beach, on an island, somewhere in the middle of the Pacific Ocean ...*

SCENE NINE

This scene splits between the court and KATIE *and* SHAHIN *on their quest.*

In court. ADRIAN *is on Zoom.*

MADDY: [*to the audience*] The storm leaves behind it a trail of destruction, but Adrian stays safe and eventually power and his internet connection is restored.

ADRIAN: You were great, Paul.

MADDY: He was brilliant. Now what?

ADRIAN: Now we have to listen to their side.

MADDY: [*to the audience*] And they talk about how they're investing in technology, not taxes. Because—well you know the argument—what happens when the wind doesn't blow and the sun doesn't shine?

PAUL: Batteries, you nongs!

MADDY: [*whispering*] Dad …!

[*To the audience*] Then they get stuck into a character attack on Dad. Accusing him of negligence, letting me go off to protests unsupervised.

PAUL: 'Child abuse?' Letting my daughter protest for her future?

MADDY: And how ugly wind farms are destroying our beautiful countryside …

PAUL: [*to* MADDY] Have they never seen a coal mine?

MADDY: But their main argument is quite simple—that it's just not their problem.

ADRIAN: But if it's not their fault, not their problem, and not their responsibility, whose responsibility is it then? Who is to be held accountable for the impact on this young girl's home and her future?

On the island somewhere in the Pacific. KATIE *and* SHAHIN *sit apart. Suddenly the tablet lights up and a video begins to play. We see the images projected on the screen.*

KATIE: Where is this from, Shahin? I didn't … I don't …

Beat.

It's a world; that is … uninhabitable. Wildfires blazing, raging seas, homes flooded, ice caps melted. Forests felled … The air clogged with smoke. The sun black.

Beat.

There's a date … [*Holding the tablet to her face*] January first, 2050.

Beat.

[*Looking up*] Shahin, look at the moon. We've been sitting here all day. The full moon is looking incredible tonight. [*Realising with a start*] It's the eclipse! We have to get this done before the eclipse! Oh no. Oh no. Oh no oh no oh no oh no …

The image on the tablet changes and it is projected onto the screen: Countdown to Total Lunar Eclipse. Eight hours, fifty-nine minutes and fifty-nine seconds ...

Well come on Shahin—what are you waiting for? Shahin? [*Shaking him*] Shahin?

Shahin?

[*Tearfully*] Shahin—I'll miss you. [*Defensively*] Hey—'ve been through a lot with this beautiful big bird … [*Correcting*] Little bird.

Back in the court.

MADDY: [*to the audience*] It's the last day of the hearing. It's a Friday. Adrian gives his summation, but he asks me to have the final word.

ADRIAN: Over to you, Maddy.

MADDY: This is a story my father used to tell me …

MADDY *and* PAUL *share a moment.* MADDY *takes a deep breath.*

And so Jack planted the magic seed deep in the earth, watered it and waited. And tended to the soil, and waited. And the next morning when he came out to check his seed's progress, there was a tiny sprout. He watered it and waited. And tended the soil and waited. And it grew. And grew. And before long an enormous beanstalk had grown, so tall, it rose all the way to the sky. And lush and green it was too. With shoots soon growing in all directions. He marvelled at its beauty.

And he didn't climb it.

He didn't search for treasure atop the bean stalk, nor seek golden geese to steal, nor giants to fight. Nor did he wield his axe to hack off its limbs for fuel.

For he knew that this beanstalk itself was the treasure.

This was the magic. The power of nature. To grow and to heal.

You have a single magic seed in your hands right now, your honour. It is up to you to help it grow.

On the island somewhere in the Pacific. SHAHIN *is lifeless and has shrunk to his original much smaller size.*

KATIE: Now what?

She panics as she spots a fin coming towards her.

Sharks! You've got to be kidding. No— [*Hugely relieved*] Dolphins! Hey! Hey! I need your help!

She races out to the dolphins.

Okay okay, I feel like a total madwoman but I really need your help. I was given these seeds from the future and I have one more and need to plant it in a total ridiculous hurry because I nearly gave up saving the planet and then my falcon died and then it shrank which is weird I know but I've still got to plant this seed in the Indian Ocean and I have no way to even get out of this island—but maybe you can help and—WOAH!

Suddenly a DOLPHIN *dives below her and before she knows it she's riding it.*

Alright, away we go! So long, Shahin and thanks for all the fish!

SCENE TEN

MADDY, ADRIAN *and* PAUL *outside the Children's Court.* KATIE *is riding a* DOLPHIN.

ADRIAN: [*on the phone*] Yes? Yes? Fantastic!

Great news—the magistrate in the Children's Court has dismissed all the charges against you. She's agreed you had a legitimate right to protest. You're free—with a caution.

PAUL: That's brilliant! Adrian thank you so much.

ADRIAN: A caution and a thousand dollar fine for damages.

PAUL: A thousand dollars? Maddy, that's a lot of pocket money you'll be paying me back.

MADDY: A thousand dollars? Dad?!

PAUL: We'll talk about it.

He embraces her tightly.

MADDY: But what about the other case—'Maddy versus the Minister'?

PAUL: This is the one, Maddy. This is what matters.

MADDY: No Dad. We have to win both cases.

ADRIAN: The judge is still deliberating. Give them time.

MADDY: But that's exactly what we're running out of …

PAUL: 'The two most powerful warriors are patience and time.' That's Tolstoy.

KATIE: And eventually, miraculously, we go down deep one last time. We are in the Indian Ocean.

MADDY *addresses the audience.*

MADDY: And so we—me and all my school friends who were there at the beginning, at those Fridays where we had striked so many times for our future on the streets of Wagga—

They're all here, all come all the way to Sydney. And so has my whole family. They walk with me. And we all walk. There's this incredible full moon out. More and more people are joining us spontaneously, the further we go, and they're all going absolutely nuts in anticipation.

KATIE: Slugs still in place as we spiral down past a myriad of sea life large and small, down deep past wrecks, past rubbish, past squid, past seahorse, through ocean forests, colours draining.

MADDY: And we end up filling the Sydney Harbour Bridge. A sea of people all crowding on the bridge. Waiting.

PAUL *addresses the audience.*

PAUL: And for a time it's as if we all hold our breath—waiting to hear how the court will respond.

MADDY: And we wait.

PAUL: Suspended in time—

MADDY: Soon we are thousands. Tens of thousands. Hundreds of thousands.

PAUL: Day turns into night—and this night—tonight it is a superb full moon shining down on us.

KATIE: And as I plant the last of the seeds deep on the floor of the Indian Ocean, all I can see above me is blackness. Am I too late? Have I failed?

MADDY: I see the moon disappearing. Little by little. Like it's blurring at the edges … What's happening?

KATIE: And I'm up. Gasping for air. The dolphins have gone. I lay on my back, floating on the ocean.

PAUL: We all turn our heads to the sky. A lunar eclipse /

ADRIAN: The super blood moon lunar eclipse.

KATIE: I look to the night sky.

MADDY: And we wait.

PAUL: We wait /

KATIE: Wait until /

PAUL: We wait until the sun, Earth and moon move into their perfect alignment.

KATIE: And then /

MADDY: Then /

PAUL: Then at long last …

MADDY: The moon shines red. / Blood red.

KATIE: A blood red moon. Perfect.

PAUL: … Exhale …

KATIE: And under the light of this magical moon …

MADDY: A wonder …

KATIE: I wonder if what I've done is enough?

PAUL: Have we done enough to convince them?

KATIE: Will these seeds do what was promised?

PAUL: How could so much possibly rest on just one decision?

KATIE: And I wonder how I'm actually going to get home now!

MADDY: Adrian's phone pings. Time to head back to court.

PAUL: We race back to court.

ADRIAN: Stand as the judge enters and delivers her verdict.

A silence while they listen …

And then they sit. Stunned.

MADDY: Did she just say what I thought she said?

PAUL: She did.

MADDY: Does that mean what I think it means?

PAUL: It does.

MADDY: Did we …?

PAUL: Yes we did.

MADDY: We won?

ADRIAN: We won.

PAUL *throws his arms up in the air in celebration.*

PAUL: [*cheering*] Woo-hoo! I'm SO proud of you, sweetheart.

ADRIAN: Congratulations to you both.

PAUL: Adrian, thank you so much.

KATIE: Suddenly I see a small catamaran coming toward me.

PAUL: [*reading the verdict*] 'A great injustice has been inflicted by the inaction of one generation of Australian adults upon the next. This court finds that the government has a legal duty of care to protect *all* its citizens, including young people, from the significant risks of climate change caused by emissions of carbon dioxide into the Earth's atmosphere. It finds the government negligent in its duty, and in compensation for the adverse impacts that will be suffered awards damages to the plaintiff.'

MADDY: Is that me?

PAUL: That's you, Maddy.

[*Reading*] 'Furthermore, the court imposes a positive obligation on the government to take immediate measures for the prevention of further impact and to mitigate against further damage.'

MADDY: So what does all that mean?

PAUL: It means we won.

TINO *appears.*

KATIE: It's Tino!!

TINO: You've done it, Katie, you've done it! Come aboard!

KATIE: And as I climb on board his vessel—

TINO: Wind and solar powered of course—

KATIE: He shows me the magic taking place around the world.

KATIE: And it is without question the most incredible sight.

MADDY: So they'll have to support renewable energy, stop building coal mines, protect forests, and basically do everything we've been asking?

TINO: We have a bird's-eye view from our satellites of what's happening.

PAUL: I think that's going to be a great place to start.

TINO: The golden seeds planted in the deserts are already beginning to grow into enormous beanstalks shooting straight up to the sky.

KATIE: With no golden goose but seven enormous golden leaves shooting out from the tops of them as they begin to reach out to the sky.

TINO: Like enormous golden beach umbrellas to cool the planet.

MADDY: But how do we know they'll actually do it?

PAUL: We don't. But this sets a precedent, Maddy. It may be our names on the case, but it's not just about us.

KATIE: And the blue seeds in the oceans—they are growing great kelp forests right across our ocean floor.

TINO: Spreading out across the seas to capture carbon and bury it deep in our waters.

KATIE: Cooling our oceans, helping our aquatic life return.

MADDY: Then the PM calls me to say they will accept the court's decision and they would like me to join them for a press conference.

KATIE: And those green seeds begin to regenerate grass all across the Earth, green shoots suddenly appearing in the most unlikely places, growing and spreading at high speed.

TINO: Taking over roads and highways, bridges and freeways, vines shooting up all over towns, winding and wrapping themselves around town halls, office blocks, climbing up city skyscrapers.

PAUL: And around the world too, governments and corporations everywhere finally start to take notice. Things are changing.

TINO: The Earth is being reborn.

PAUL: The polar ice caps stop melting. The fires stop burning. The Earth stops its relentless warming.

> KATIE *and* TINO *hold hands as they look out in wonder at what is taking place around them.*

KATIE: Incredible.

PAUL: And the dolphins celebrate.

PAUL *puts his arm around* MADDY *and holds her tightly.*

MADDY: And / we did it.
PAUL: / You did it.
KATIE: / We did it.
TINO: You did it.

EPILOGUE

Music: a gloriously upbeat celebratory song begins to build as they continue ... 'Mr Blue Sky' by the Electric Light Orchestra would be perfect. If a recording is to be played, go with the Triple J Live at the Wireless Version by Alex the Astronaut, 2020.

PAUL: And we all head back home.
KATIE: Hey Maddy. Good to see you again. I hear you've been busy since I saw you last.
MADDY: Just a bit! I hear you went away somewhere?
KATIE: I needed to get out of town and find my place in the world. [*Studying* MADDY] You've changed since the last time I saw you … You've grown for starters.
MADDY: I guess saving the planet does that! [*Looking closely at* KATIE] You've changed too …
KATIE: You're not the only one who had some growing to do.

They look at each other. And smile.

PAUL: And we all live happily ever after.
KATIE: The princess saves the frog. Frogs. All of them.
PAUL: Even that endangered southern corroboree frog.
TINO: And the Manumea bird.
MADDY: And the bilbies, and black flanked rock wallabies and pink cockatoos.
PAUL: And the platypus.
TINO: And the sand gazelles.
MADDY: And the Siberian tigers.
KATIE: And the Andean deer.
PAUL: And the polar bears.
TINO: And the gorillas.
MADDY: And the koalas too!

PAUL: Yes, definitely the koalas.

MADDY: The planet, *our* planet, is saved and our future is safe.

Maybe they all sing together here. In any case the vocals shine through at this point as MADDY *and* KATIE *dance. It's a joyous release. A party. They start inviting the audience on stage to dance with them by now. Then the music cuts off suddenly. House lights go on.*

MADDY: [*stepping forward*] And maybe there is a Planet B waiting for us in the future. I don't know about you—but I don't want to wait and find out. So we will keep speaking out. We will keep shouting at the top of our lungs: 'Our world is on fire—do something.'

PAUL: And we will keep dreaming and telling stories until enough is done to *truly* save our future.

MADDY *sits back down in the centre of the stage. She is now in the exact same position, in the same costume, and with the exact same sign as she had at the end of Act One, Scene One. The sign reads: 'Unless someone like you cares a whole awful lot. Nothing is going to get better. It's not. Dr Seuss.'*

MADDY: Who's with me?
Who's with me?
Who's with me?

THE END